The Wild Life.

A little bit lost.

For ~~Quo~~ Arthur, with love xx

Omnibus Books
an imprint of Scholastic Australia Pty Ltd
(ABN 11 000 614 577)
PO Box 579, Gosford NSW 2250.
www.scholastic.com.au

Part of the Scholastic Group • Sydney • Auckland • New York • Toronto • London • Mexico City • New Delhi • Hong Kong • Buenos Aires • Puerto Rico

Published by Scholastic Australia in 2023.
Text copyright © Laura Bunting, 2023.
Illustrations copyright © Philip Bunting, 2023.
The moral rights of Laura Bunting have been asserted.
The moral rights of Philip Bunting have been asserted.

All rights reserved. No part of this publication may be reproduced or transmitted in any form or by any means, electronic or mechanical, including photocopying, recording, storage in an information retrieval system, or otherwise, without the prior written permission of the publisher, unless specifically permitted under the Australian Copyright Act 1968 as amended.

A catalogue record for this book is available from the National Library of Australia

ISBN: 978-1-76129-171-5

Printed in China by Asia Pacific Offset. Scholastic Australia's policy, in association with Asia Pacific Offset, is to use papers that are renewable and made efficiently from wood grown in responsibly managed forests, so as to minimise its environmental footprint.

10 9 8 7 6 5 4 3 2 1   23 24 25 26 27 / 2

Queensland Government   This project is supported by the Queensland Government through Arts Queensland.

We acknowledge the traditional custodians of the land on which we live and work, and pay respect to the Gubbi Gubbi nation. We pay respects to the Elders of the community and extend our recognition to their descendants.
Laura and Philip Bunting.

Story by Laura Bunting.
Illustrations by Philip Bunting.

The Wild Life!

A little bit lost.

An Omnibus book from
Scholastic Australia.

PART 1

(In which Roo has babies... weird babies)

Roo was enjoying the most thrilling sleep of her life. In her dreams, she was floating, no, not floating... flying!
She darted with the dragonflies, cruised with the kingfishers and barrel-rolled with the butterflies. She whooped and whee'd as she felt the wind whistle past her ears.

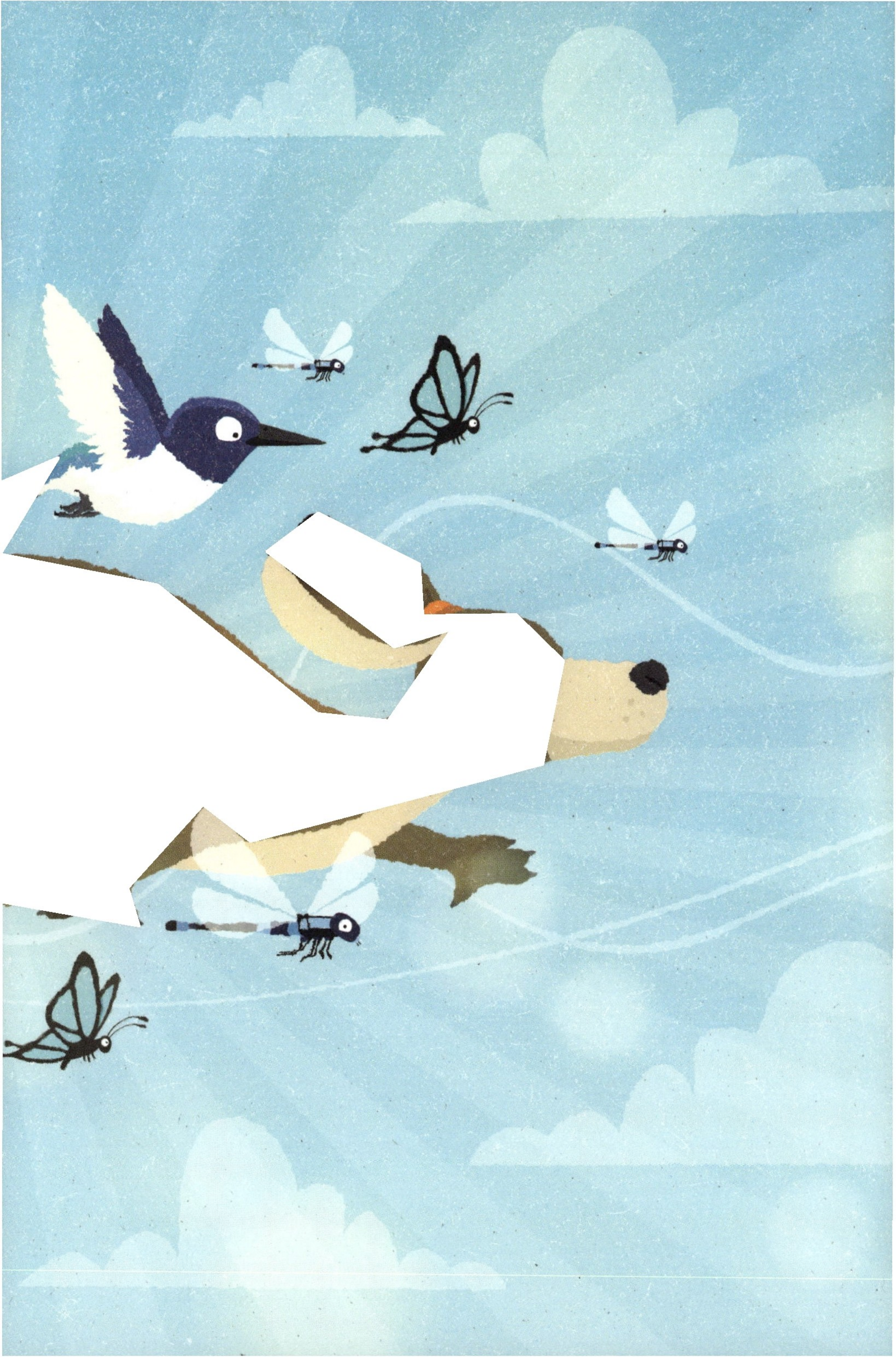

All at once, a strange sound roused her from her slumber. Shrieking. In. Her. Ear.
"Eeee! Eeee! Eeeee!"

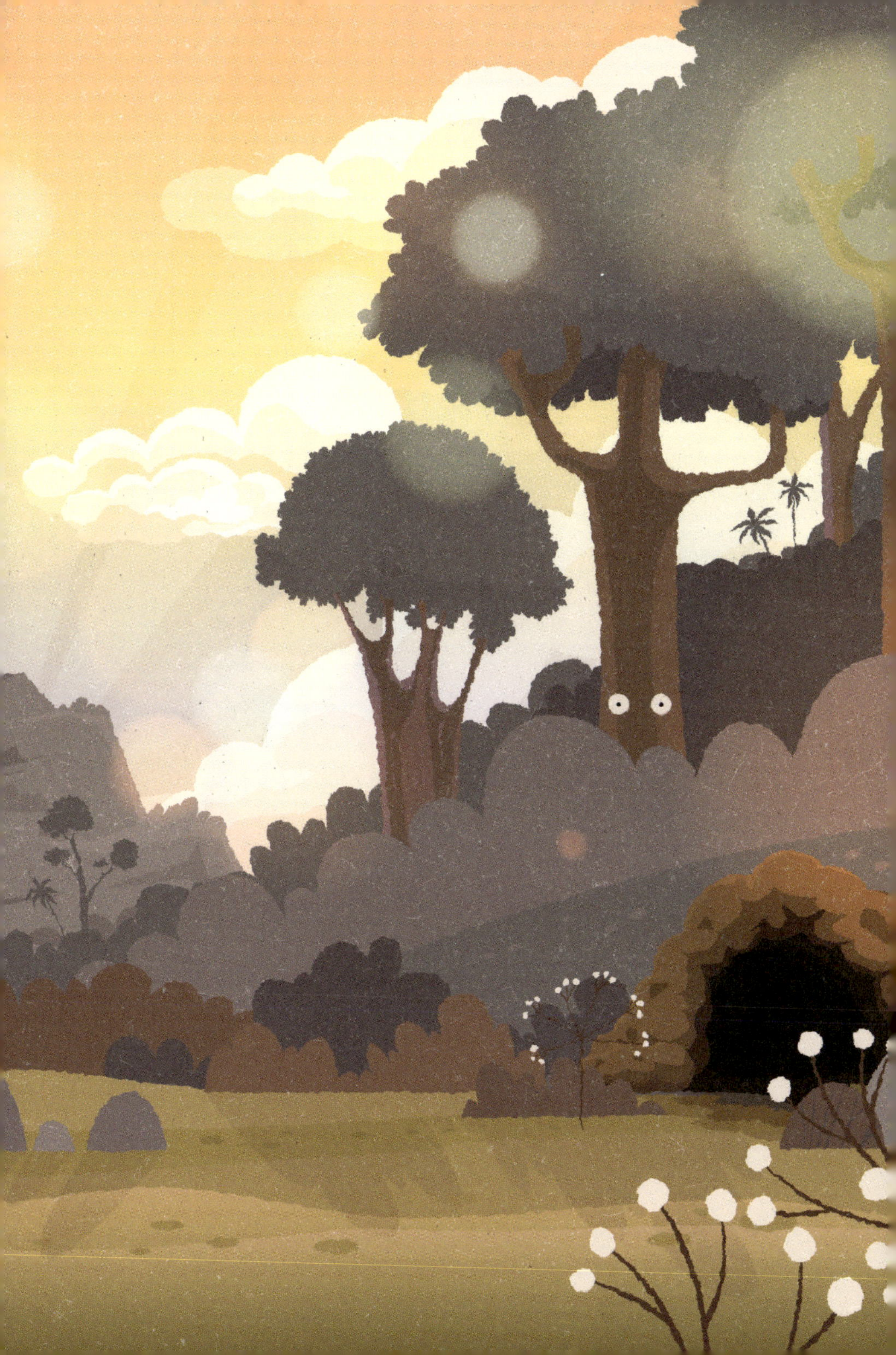

"Wake up, Wombat!"
she mumbled drowsily.
"You're dreaming about
zombie snails, again!"

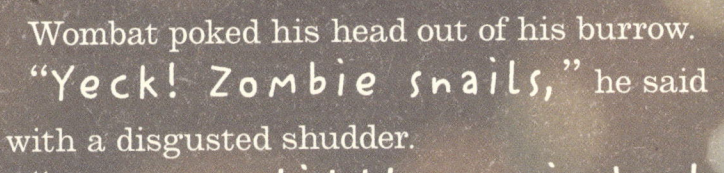

Wombat poked his head out of his burrow. "Yeck! Zombie snails," he said with a disgusted shudder. "Creepy little weirdos! But I've been up for ages, so the sleep shrieks aren't coming from me, for once," he added, before retreating back into his burrow.

The bushes next to Roo rustled. Quokka emerged, dishevelled and cranky.

"Oi! Some of us need our Cutie Sleep you know! What's all this rack-eeehht?!" he yelped, as he was met with a most unexpected sight.

"Roo! You've... you've..."

...given birth!"
he cried. "Yeck! Babies!"
he added with a disgusted shudder.
"Creepy little weirdos."

Roo's eyes shot down to her pouch and there, staring back up at her, were two babies. There was a third on her shoulder, shrieking in her ear.

"Eeee eeee eee ee!"

"I'm a... mother?" she mumbled. "Oh!" she exclaimed as she inspected her joeys. Joeys with... feathers, beaks and claws. "They're beautiful! But... I don't think I did it right!"

Roo's brain swirled with half-asleep nonsense:

Is this what kangaroo babies look like?

Tweet?

Did I metamorphose into a **bird** while I was **sleeping**?

Eeeeeeee! Are joeys always this noisy?

Within a few seconds, she fainted.
Her brain simply couldn't cope with
so many silly thoughts at once.

Eeeee!
Eee!

"Hey, Wombat!" called Quokka. "Come see Roo's *weird babies.*"

Eee!

"Roo had babies?" said Wombat.
"Well, that is a surprise!"

For a moment, he lost himself in a daydream, imagining the kind of Fun Uncle (or Funcle, as he decided he would be known) he was going to make.

Fun Times with Funcle Wombat.

Danger! Danger! Danger!

Day 1: All the dangers.

Day 2: How to burrow.

Day 3: Geometry.

Ear-piercing shrieking interrupted his daydream.

"Well, all babies are a bit weird, Quokka," said Wombat, raising his voice over the noise. "But I'm sure they're lovel-*eeeek!*" he yelped, as he emerged from his burrow and caught sight of Roo and her very, very weird babies.

Eeeeeee! Eeeee! Eeee!

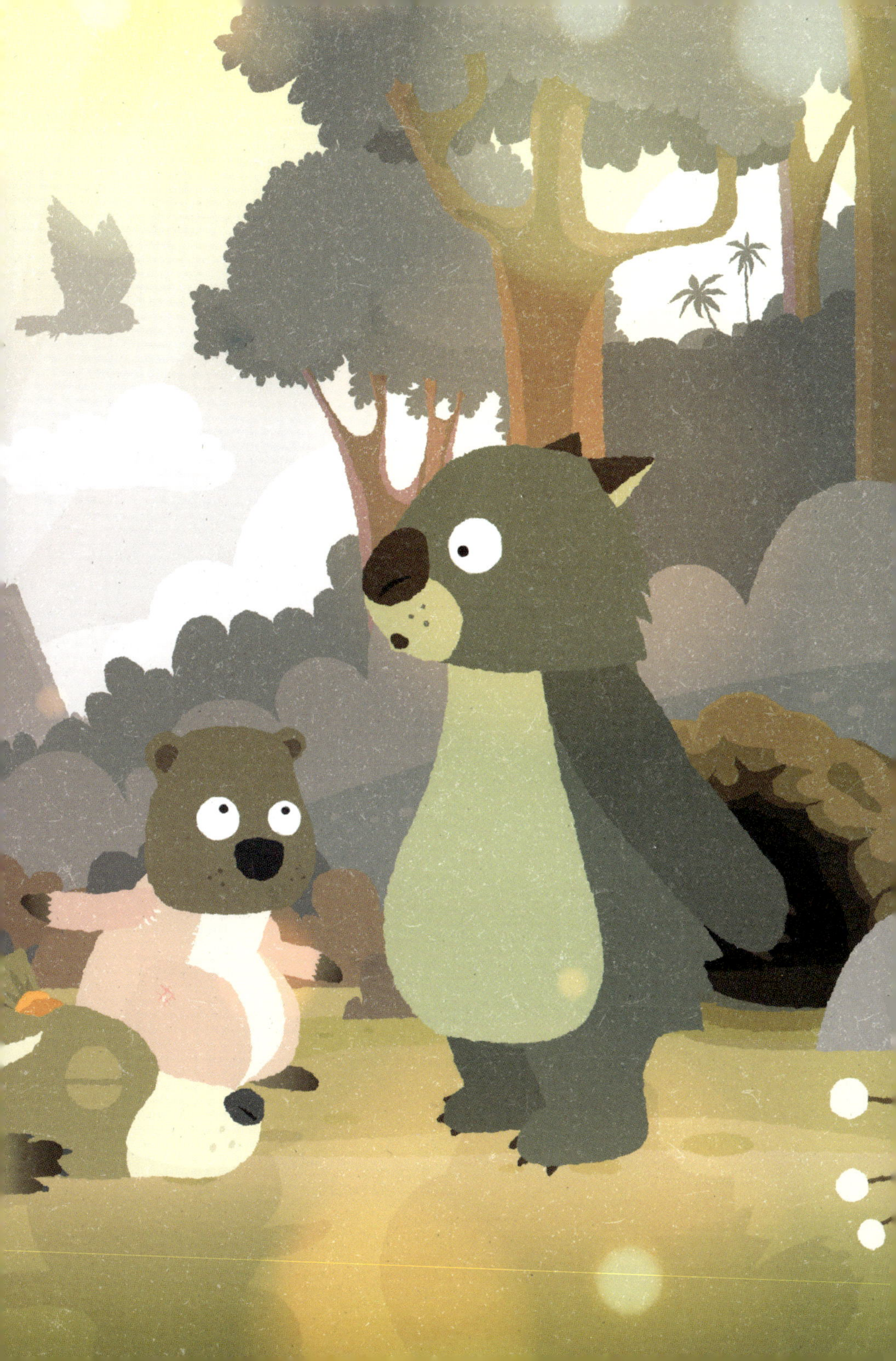

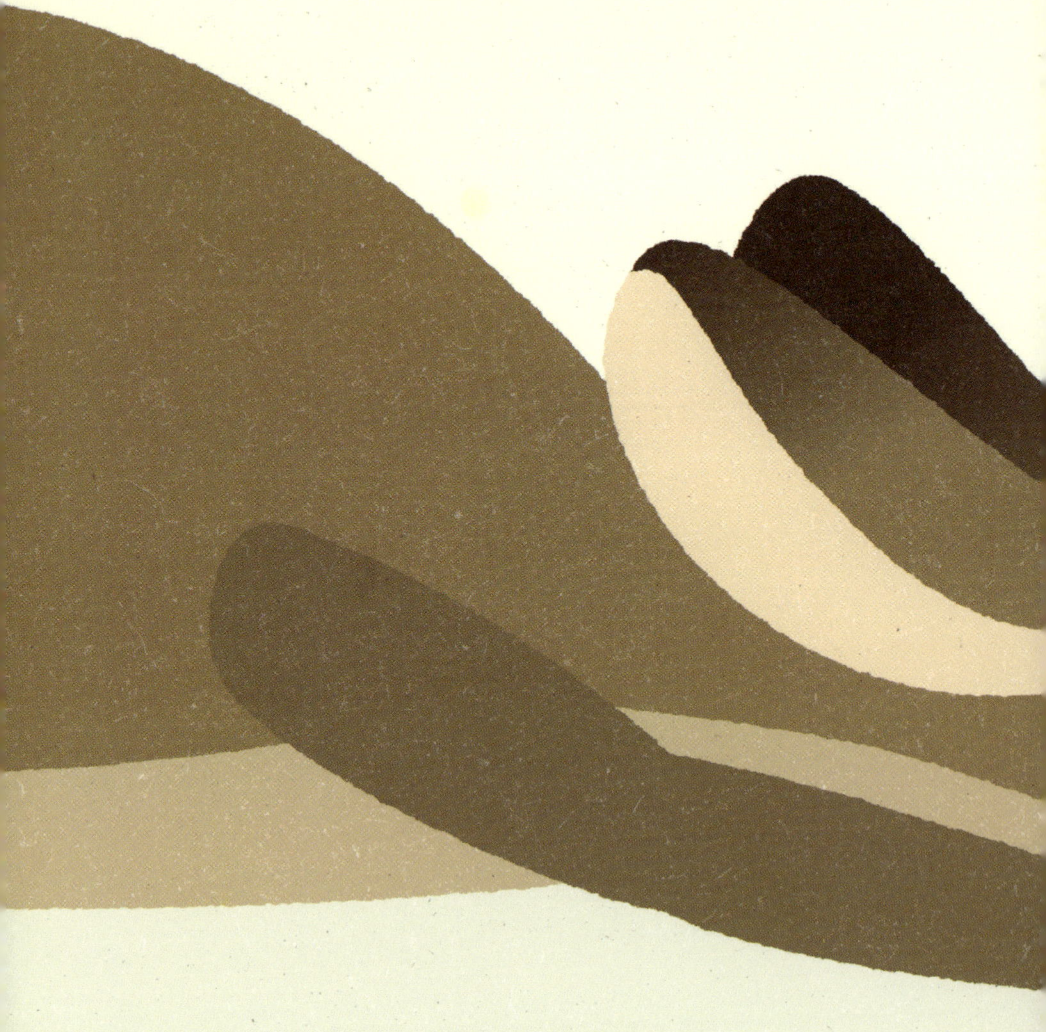

PART 2

(In which they find a dirty clue)

"Poor Roo," said Wombat, crushing some gum leaves and waving them under her nose.

As Roo blearily opened her eyes, Wombat spoke slowly. "Roo, for reasons I can't explain, you have babies in your pouch, but don't panic, they're not your babies."

Eeee! Eee!
Eeee! Eee!
Eee!

"Of course they are her babies!" gasped Quokka. "They are in her pouch!"

"But these are *bird babies*," replied Wombat. "And Roo is not a bird."
"Oh," said Quokka.

"So, kangaroos don't start out as scrawny little chickens? Are you sure? Imagine if frogs said the same thing about their babies!

Don't look! That weird little fish thinks I'm its mother.

Mama!

If these really **are bird babies**, then where are the eggs they hatched from?"

"I- I- well, I don't know," stammered Wombat. "But I know for a fact they're not Roo's. They must be lost. Maybe they fell out of a nest."

Eeee!

"I just can't think properly with all this noise!" he yelled as the chicks continued their shrill shrieks.

Eeeee! Eee! Eeeeeeeeee!

Eeee! Eee!

Eee!

Eee! Eee!

Eee!

"They're **so loud!**" cried Quokka. "How do we make them stop?"

"We need to **find their parents**," shouted Wombat.

"But **how?**" yelled Quokka.

"**What?**" shouted Wombat.

"**Hoo!**" boomed a loud voice from above.

Eee! Eeee! Eeeeeeee! Eee!

Eeeeee!
Eeee!
Eee!

"Who...?"
Wombat and Quokka looked up.
Owl gave them a dirty look.
Then she gave them something
even dirtier for so rudely
disrupting her sleep.

"It's in my eye!"
"It's in my eye!"
squealed Quokka.
Wombat gave Owl
a disapproving look.

Owl shrugged, then made some pointing motions with her wings.

"Oh, not charades!" moaned Quokka. "I'm terrible at charades. Is it a stick? A stone? A sticky stone?"

Owl sighed, then swooped down and pointed at some curious markings in the dirt, before returning to her branch.

"Oh look! Owl has written us a clue," said Quokka. "It looks like a W. What words start with a W . . ." he pondered. "Wuh, Wuh, Wuh . . . wittchety grub, wizard, willie wagtail!" he cried.

"That's it! We must be looking for a wittchety grub – who also happens to be a wizard – riding a willie wagtail . . . They will direct us to the parents of these chicks!"

Onward!

"These aren't letters," said Roo. "They're footprints. I think Owl is telling us that these tracks were made by the chicks' parents."

"That is a footprint?" gasped Quokka. "Of . . . a bird?! But, but, that footprint is bigger than my head. It's bigger than me! Which means the bird attached to this foot must be . . . ginormous . . . humongous . . . enormous . . .

gimongmous!"

he squealed, as the colour drained from his body, until he looked like a hairy little ghost.

"If we follow these tracks, we'll be able to reunite the chicks with their parents!" said Roo excitedly. "Let's go!"

"You two have fun!" said Quokka. "Make sure to send me a postcard!"

"You're not coming?" said Roo.

"No way!" said Quokka. "If that giant freak of nature sees us with its chicks and assumes we stole them, well, you two are big enough to stand some chance of survival. As for little old me? It will gobble me in one go, like a furry screaming jelly bean. No thank you! I'm staying right here."

"Excellent idea!" said Roo. "That way, if the parents come back here looking for the chicks, you can tell them which way we went."

And with that frightening image in mind, Quokka placed a shrieking chick under his arm and reluctantly joined Wombat and Roo on the quest.

Eee!
Eee!

Eeee!

Eee!
Eee!

PART 3

(In which Wombat learns how **not** to be a Funcle)

Eee!

Eee!

Eeee!

The group walked for many hours. They navigated unfamiliar landscapes.

Eeeee!

Eee!

And encountered unfamiliar creatures.

They hadn't let the chicks out of their sight. Especially Wombat.

Eee!

"Stay close! Don't run! Watch out!" he yelled in a fluster as he tried, quite unsuccessfully, to keep the cheeky chicks under control. He certainly wasn't being the *Funcle* he imagined. *More like an unfuncle*, he thought to himself disappointedly.

"I feel like the only word I have said since we set off is '**no**'," said Wombat, miserably.

No!

No!

Oooh, brownies!

No!

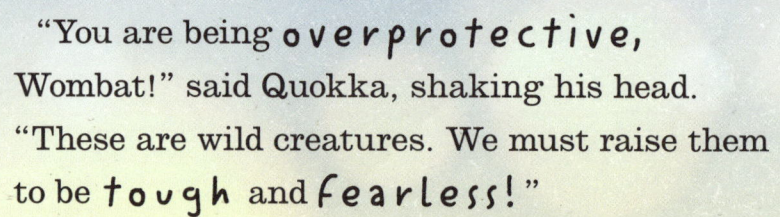

"You are being overprotective, Wombat!" said Quokka, shaking his head. "These are wild creatures. We must raise them to be tough and fearless!"

"Oh, like you?" said Roo with a friendly wink. "You're a wild creature, and you weren't so fearless this morning."

"Exactly!" said Quokka. "But I will raise my baby to be different! She will not have any of my faults."

Eee?

"No, Pedro! Don't eat that! Pink butterflies will give you beakache. Spit it out! Yuck!" cried Wombat. "Sorry, Quokka, but I'm not taking parenting advice from an animal that throws its babies at predators to escape!"

"**How dare you!**" gasped Quokka. "Our beautiful mothers do not throw us at predators to escape.

Best of luck, Buttercup! Love you!

They release us out of their pouch very gently while they run away and save themselves. It makes us . . . resilient."

Wombat eyed Quokka suspiciously, then picked up his chick and Quokka's chick and cuddled them close.

"Relax, Wombat," said Quokka. "Parenting is easy. I bet I can do it with my eyes closed!"

And with that, he took his chick from Wombat, placed it in front of him and closed his eyes.

When he slowly opened them again, he saw his chick, just where he left it. "Ha! See? Easy!" he said. "Aww look, she's even made a friend!"

"That's **not a friend!**" shrieked Wombat. "That's a quoll!"

"It's pronounced **troll**," said Quokka with a knowing smile, "and they only exist in **fairytales!**"

"Not troll, **quoll!**" cried Wombat. "Imagine a very vicious cat and a very vicious fox had a very vicious baby. That's a quoll!"

"Ack!" cried Quokka.

"**Gwendolyn, darling, run!**"

Realising that his chick didn't understand, Quokka did something so surprising he even surprised himself. He slapped his bulbous belly so hard it wiggled and jiggled like a plate of meat jelly.

Wobble. Wobble.

Quoll spied the beefy bonanza,
did a quick calculation, then suddenly
changed course. Quokka yelped, grabbed
his chick, then hopped and scurried
through the shallow water.

As he launched himself towards the
safety of a small burrow, he shouted
teasingly to Quoll:

"Yum yum yum, come bite my juicy..."

bum!"

Quokka shrieked, as he realised with horror that his round rump was just too plump to fit through the burrow's opening.

PART 4

(In which Wombat's rump comes to the rescue)

Quokka's brief life flashed
before his eyes as he realised he
had just served up his beautiful bottom
on a platter, like a succulent Sunday roast.

"At least I kept you safe," whispered Quokka, smiling at his little chick.

So I have a new business idea, hear me out. We make eggs. We also make milk...

He heard footsteps splashing through the water towards him and braced himself for the bite . . .

. . . but what he felt instead was something very hard colliding with his bottom at great speed. The crash jolted him inside the burrow.

Eeeee!

Ponk!

He spun around only to see Wombat's smiling face. "Wombat!" he cried. "What are you doing?" "Saving your rump!" Wombat said with a wink.

"Oh, you beautiful creature, thank you! But, what about *your* rump?" cried Quokka. "We have to get you in here before Quoll bites you!"

"She already is!" said Wombat.
"No! No! Nooooooooooooo!"
wailed Quokka, collapsing to his knees.

"You sacrificed your
own life for mine? I will never
forget you. I will hold you in my
arms until you go, sweet Wombie."

"It's okay, Quokka, I'm fine!" said Wombat. "My backside is **bite-proof**. I can't feel a thing."

We make custard! What do you think...?

Too cute! Can we keep it?

"Bite-proof?" repeated Quokka slowly. He tried to process this information but it got stuck in his brain, somewhere between Quite Impressed and Terribly Jealous. "That is ... Incredible! Fantastic! Brilliant! And ...

Very Unfair!" he shouted. Quokka's feelings never shifted gradually. They struck like lightning — shocking, intense and best to watch from a safe distance.

#@*%!

"Why don't I have a bite-proof bottom?" he yelled, at no-one in particular. "I am just a tinier, cuter, more delicious version of you, after all. I really should be bite-proof all over!"

"I suppose that would make you a qurtle or an armadokka," said Wombat with a smile.

Fig 1: Qurtle.
Biteproofus Notcutieus.

Fig 2: Armadokka.
*Smoothontheinsideus
Crunchyontheoutsideum.*

Quokka laughed heartily and hugged his friend's face again. "You're funny, Wombie," he said, flashing once again from rage to joy in an instant.

Outside, they heard loud thumping, shuffling and then, silence.

"You can come out now!" called Roo.

"I think my thumping scared Quoll away. But she'll be back soon enough, so we should make a move, and quickly!"

PART 5

(In which danger is everywhere)

The dangers kept coming, thick and fast. Quokka, Wombat and Roo were in Survival Mode every minute as they worked tirelessly to keep their chicks out of Harm's Way.

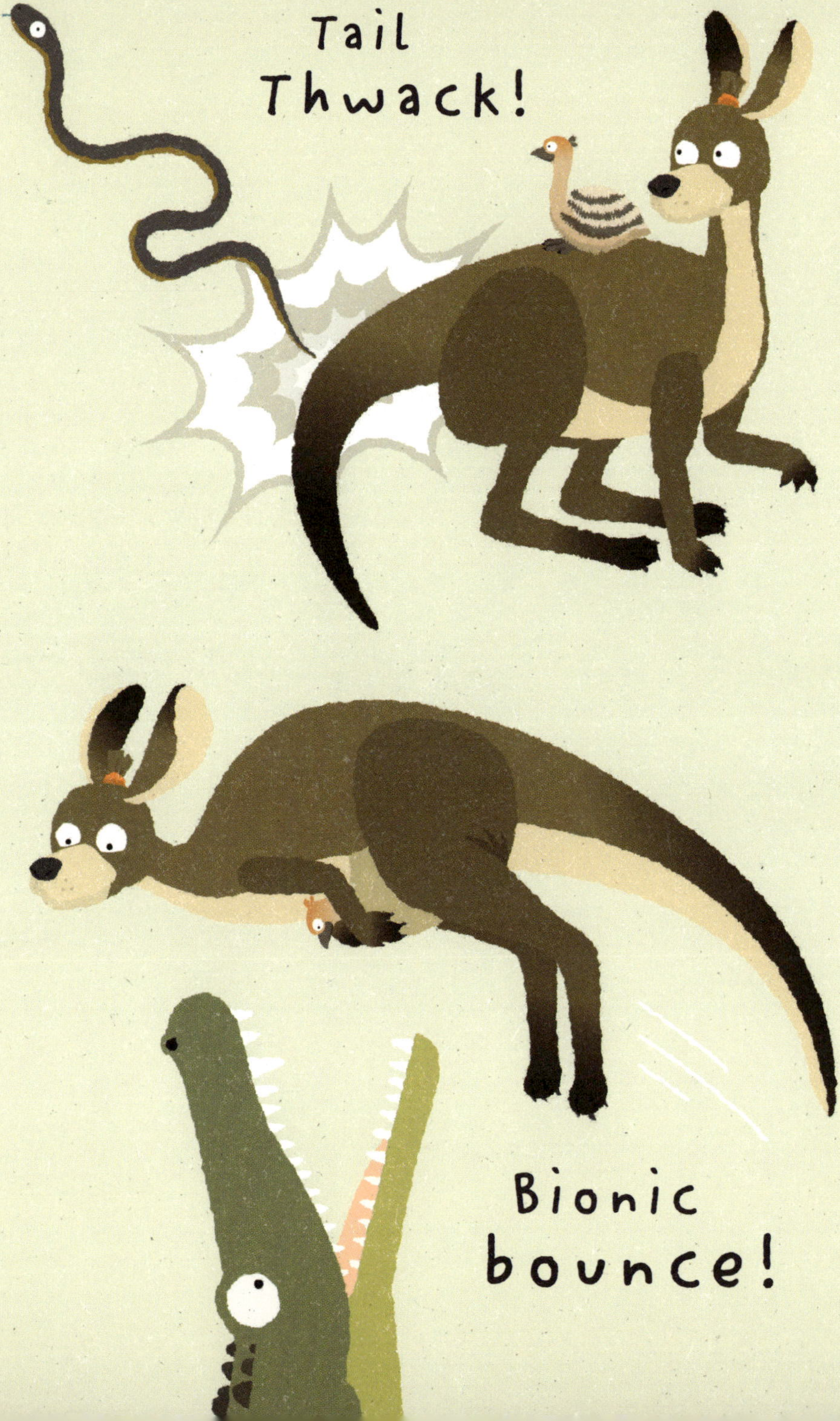
Tail Thwack!
Bionic bounce!

K.O. Kick!

Dynamite dig!

Super-sprint!

Boo... cough cough.

Rock-hard-rump!

Camouflage!

Camouflage!

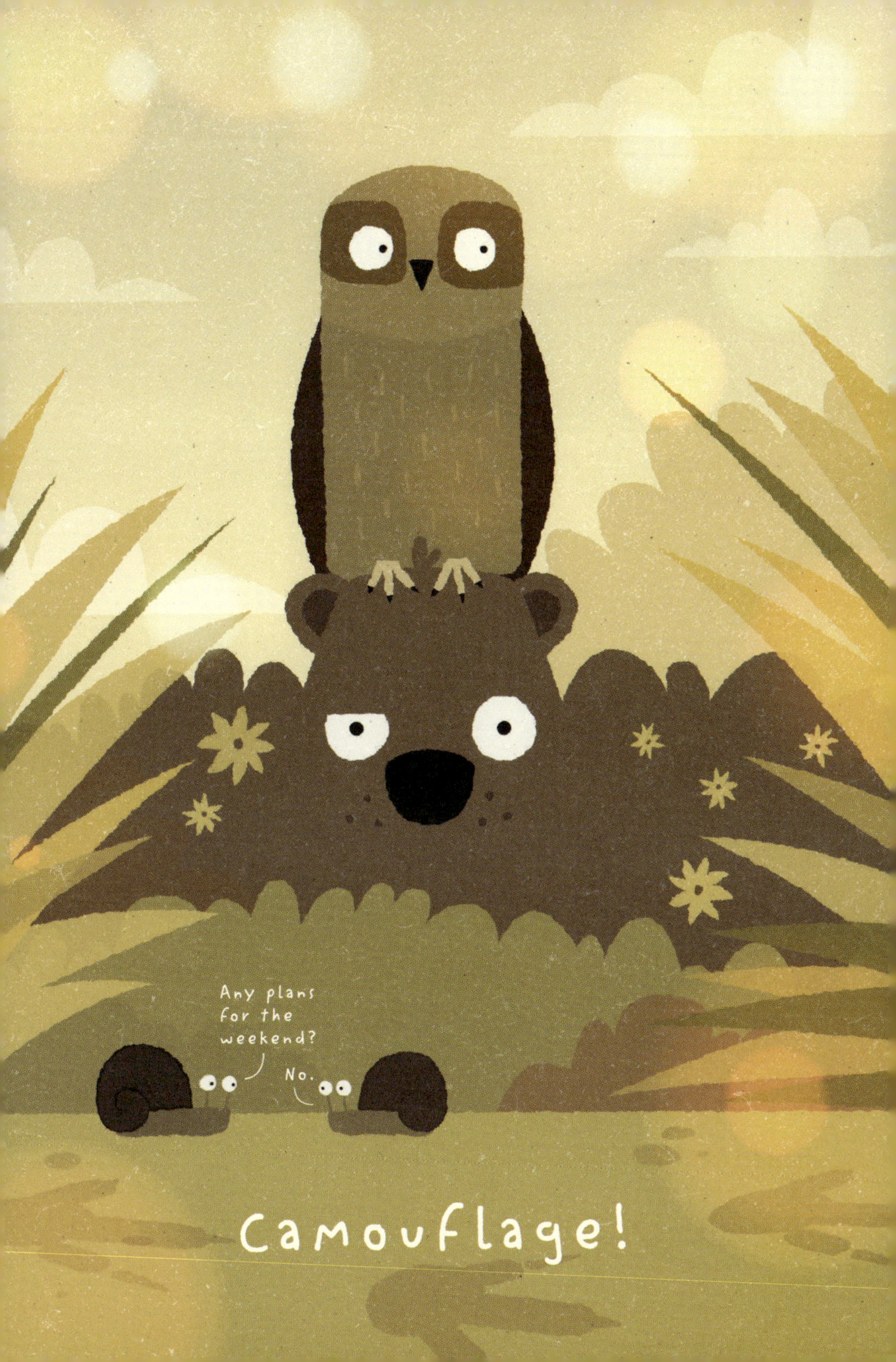

Camouflage!

As the sun sunk into the horizon, they collapsed into a heap, utterly exhausted. Quokka sighed wearily as he curled up next to Wombat and Roo. "I've been looking forward to this all day!" he said. "Night night!"

Eeee!

Zzzz

But little did they know, that their greatest battle had just begun.

K.O. Kick!

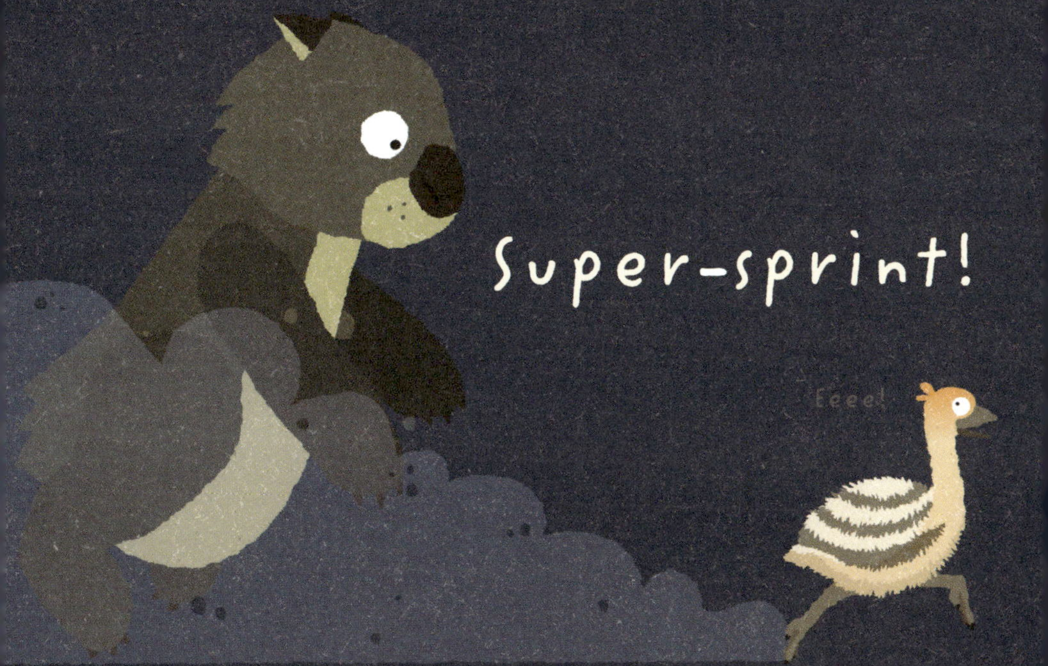

Super-sprint!

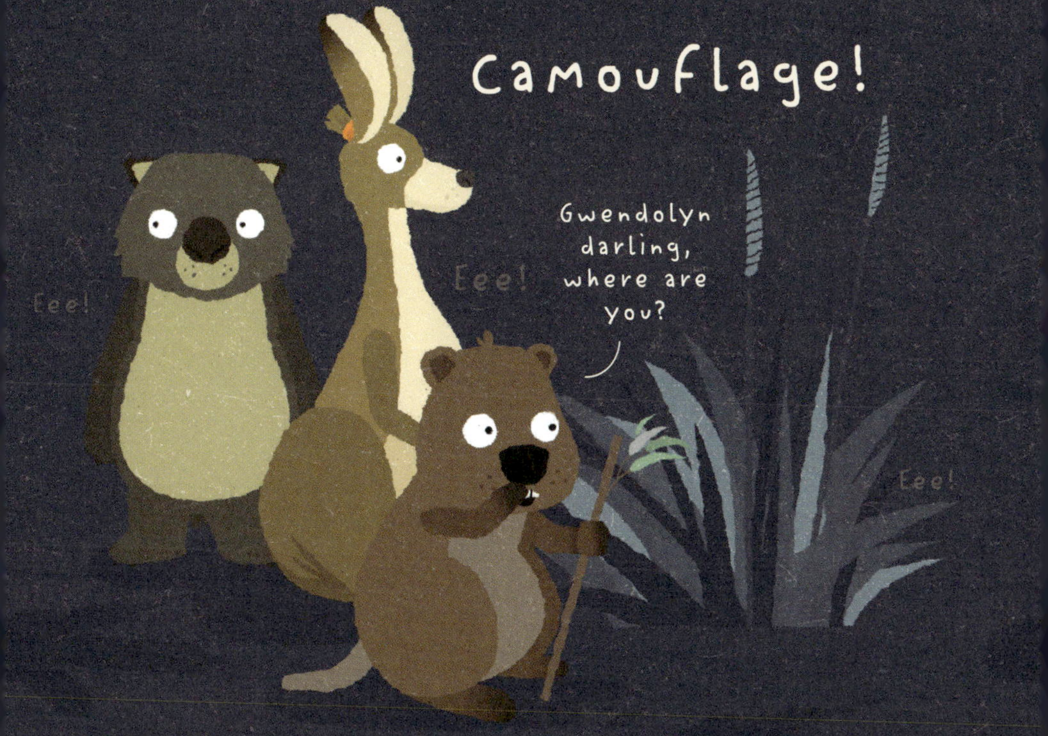

Camouflage!

Just as the group finally closed their eyes, the sun rose, the dawn chorus began and the chicks were cheeping for breakfast.

"Somebody feed them!" said Quokka wearily.

"What do they eat?" said Wombat.

"I've seen some birds vomit up food for their chicks," said Roo.

"That is yucky and is definitely not happening!" said Quokka.

"I'll hop ahead and see if I can find something for them," said Roo. But a few hops later, she stopped. "Oh no!" she cried.

"The tracks have disappeared!"

Wombat started to sniff. And sniff. And sniff. "For goodness sake, Wombat, blow your nose!" snapped Quokka. "I'm sorry, my friend," he added quietly. "I'm just very tired."

"I'm sniffing out which way they went," said Wombat.

"Wait, so you have a bite-proof bottom and super awesome sense of smell?" said Quokka.
"I do!" replied Wombat. "But why are you saying it like it's a bad thing?"

"Because, in Life's Lottery of Cool Skills, some creatures get an unfair amount of the good stuff. While others, like me, get nothing!" wailed Quokka.

Life's Lottery of Cool Skills.

Winner / Loser

Wedgie.
- ✓ Massive!
- ✓ Terrifying!
- ✓ Super-sight.
- ✓ Huge talons.
- ✓ Can fly!

Platypus.
- ✓ Ancient mammal.
- ✓ Venomous spur.
- ✓ Lays eggs and produces milk!
- ✓ Solid business plan.

Wombat.
- ✓ Bite-proof rump.
- ✓ Dynamite digging.
- ✓ Super-sniff.
- ✓ Cubic poop.
- ✓ Lovely face.

Dingo.
- ✓ Grreat grrowl.
- ✓ Pack hunter.
- ✓ Excellent model for costume.
- ✓ Frighteningly fast.

Me.
- ✓ Camouflage.

Croc.
- ✓ So many Teeth!
- ✓ Death roll!
- ✓ Amazing smile.
- ✓ Haunts dreams.
- ✓ Ate dinosaurs.

"That's not true, Quokka," said Wombat placing his paw on Quokka's shoulder. "You know, sometimes we can spend so long admiring someone else's gifts, we forget to unwrap our own."

"I know! I make that mistake every Christmas morning!" snapped Quokka. "What's your point?"

"My point is, you're only counting
my blessings. Don't forget
to count your own!" said Wombat.
"Okay, fine," said Quokka.
"I'll count my blessings..."

Blessing 1:
Round.

Blessing 2:
Squishy.

Blessing 3:
Delicious.

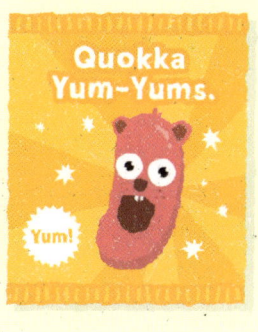

But guess what? They're not actually blessings
unless you happen to be a marshmallow!"
"I've been impressed with your camouflage
skills," said Wombat, encouragingly.
"Pssht," scoffed Quokka. "I was born
the same colour as rocks and dirt.
It's hardly impressive!"

"Well, maybe you just haven't discovered it yet," said Wombat. Then he lowered his nose to the ground and sniffed again. "That way!" he cried, pointing towards a patch of dense forest at the foot of a distant hill.

As they reached the forest, Wombat continued to sniff, and sniff and sniff. "There are so many new smells in here. I'm losing the scent... Hey! Stop prodding me, Quokka! It's not helping," he snapped.

Wombat raised his head, only to see **Quokka** and Roo gaping up into a tree. There, nearing the canopy, were their chicks, curled up in the tail of a . . .

python!

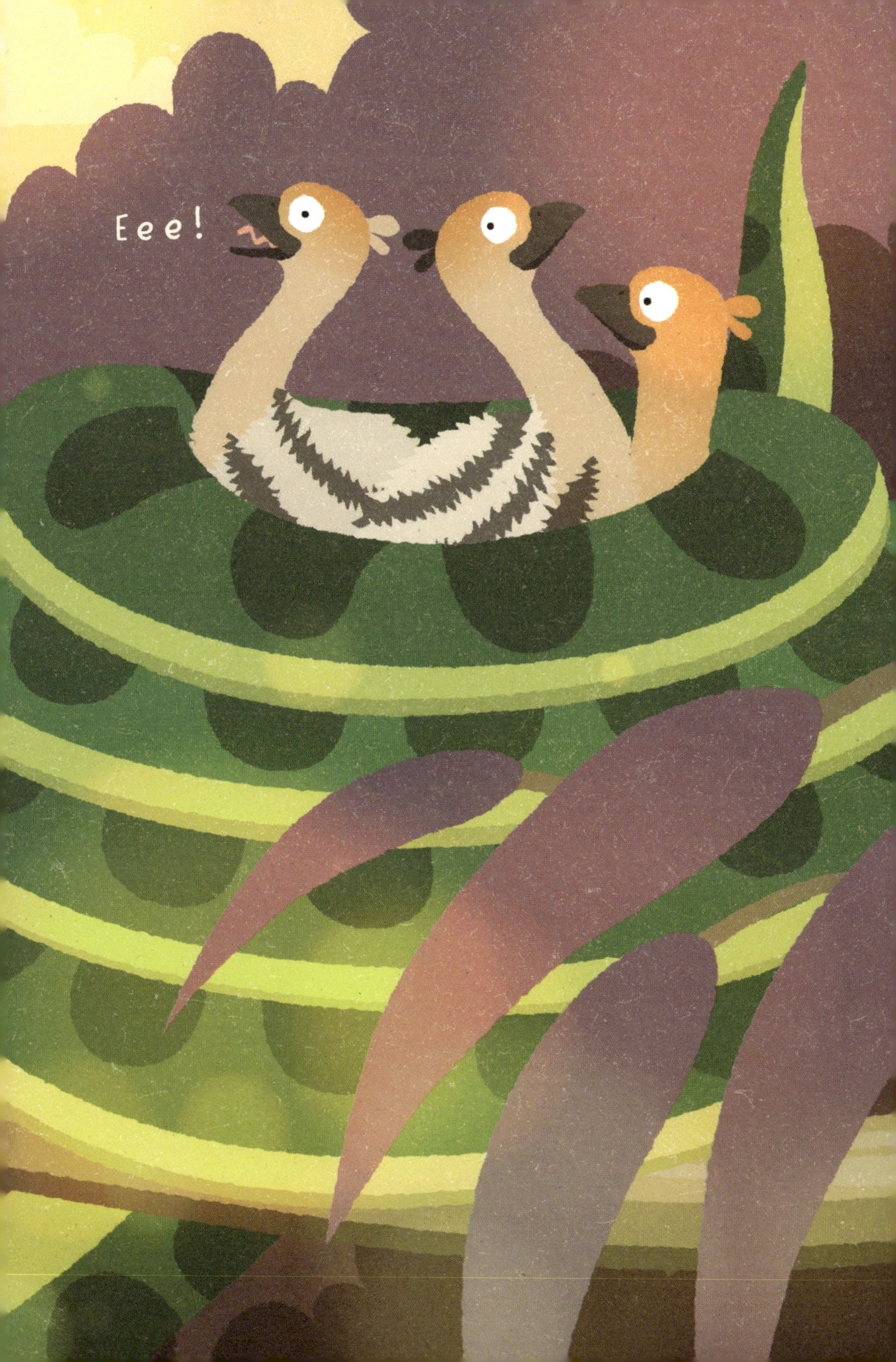
Eee!

PART 6

(In which they meet a super roo)

"Whadowedo whadowedo whadowedo?" shrieked Quokka. "Our babies are doomed! None of us can climb!"

"I can climb," came a voice from a branch overhead. And then a creature emerged from behind the leaves. It looked a lot like Roo but also a lot n o t like Roo.

"Oh, thank goodness!" cried Wombat. "Our chicks are in terrible danger. Can you climb to the top of this tree and save them, please!"

The creature scurried effortlessly up the tree onto the highest branch until he was a small blurry dot.

Then, just as suddenly, he stepped off the branch and started falling . . .

and falling . . .

and falling.

And then, with an impossibly soft thud, he landed.
"Whoa!" they all said.

"Sorry, can't help you," said the creature.

"Ohhhh!" they all whined in disappointment.

"But, you just climbed up there. Of course you can help!" added Quokka.

"Okay, what I meant to say is . . .

I won't help you.

That python has been eyeing me up for her lunch for days. Your chicks are doing me a big favour. She will soon be full and I can finally relax! Today is my lucky day."

"You're a monster!" gasped Quokka.
"No. I. Am. A. Tree. Roo," he said, slowly.
"Wait, you're a kangaroo, like me?" said Roo.
"No, I am not an Ordinary Roo like you.
I'm a Tree Roo. Which is much more . . .
super. I mean, look at me!

I have these Long **Muscly Arms** for climbing and swinging.

And Very **Excellent Thumbs** which let me climb and hold stuff.

And check out these **Amazing Legs.** Unlike **Ordinary** Roos, I can walk forwards and **backwards.** You see? I am packed with **super awesomeness.**"

"That is Super," said Roo quietly. And for the first time in her life, she felt very, very Ordinary indeed.

A terrifying **booming** noise rumbled through the forest. Quokka was so startled he blacked out.

When he opened his eyes again, he was perched high on a branch, right next to the python.

Eee! Eee! Eee!

"Eeeeeeee!" squealed Quokka, teetering precariously on the branch. "What the... How the... Why am I in a tree?"

Eee! Eee! Eee!

"You climbed, Quokka!" shouted Wombat. "You found your special inner gift. Your instinct!"

"Now is not the time to call me stinky!" snapped Quokka.

"No, not stinky . . . your **instinct**. It's **your gift from Nature.** Something you can do without even thinking about it," shouted Wombat. "Baby birds aren't taught to fly. They leap out of the nest and their bodies know exactly what to do . . . thanks to instinct."

"**Quokka! The chicks!**" cried Roo.

Eee! Eee! Eee!

"**Daddy's here, babies!**" shouted Quokka. Then, making sure not to look down, he hopped, slowly but steadily, along the branch before coming face-to-face with Python.

"Sssswweeet, juiccccy, moussssey," she hissed, releasing the chicks in favour of the mega mouseburger in front of her. They scurried into Quokka's open arms. He hugged them tight, looked them in the eye and said: "It's time to follow your instincts . . .

Eee! Eee!

Eee!

Fly, my little darlings!"

And with that, he let them go.

PART 7

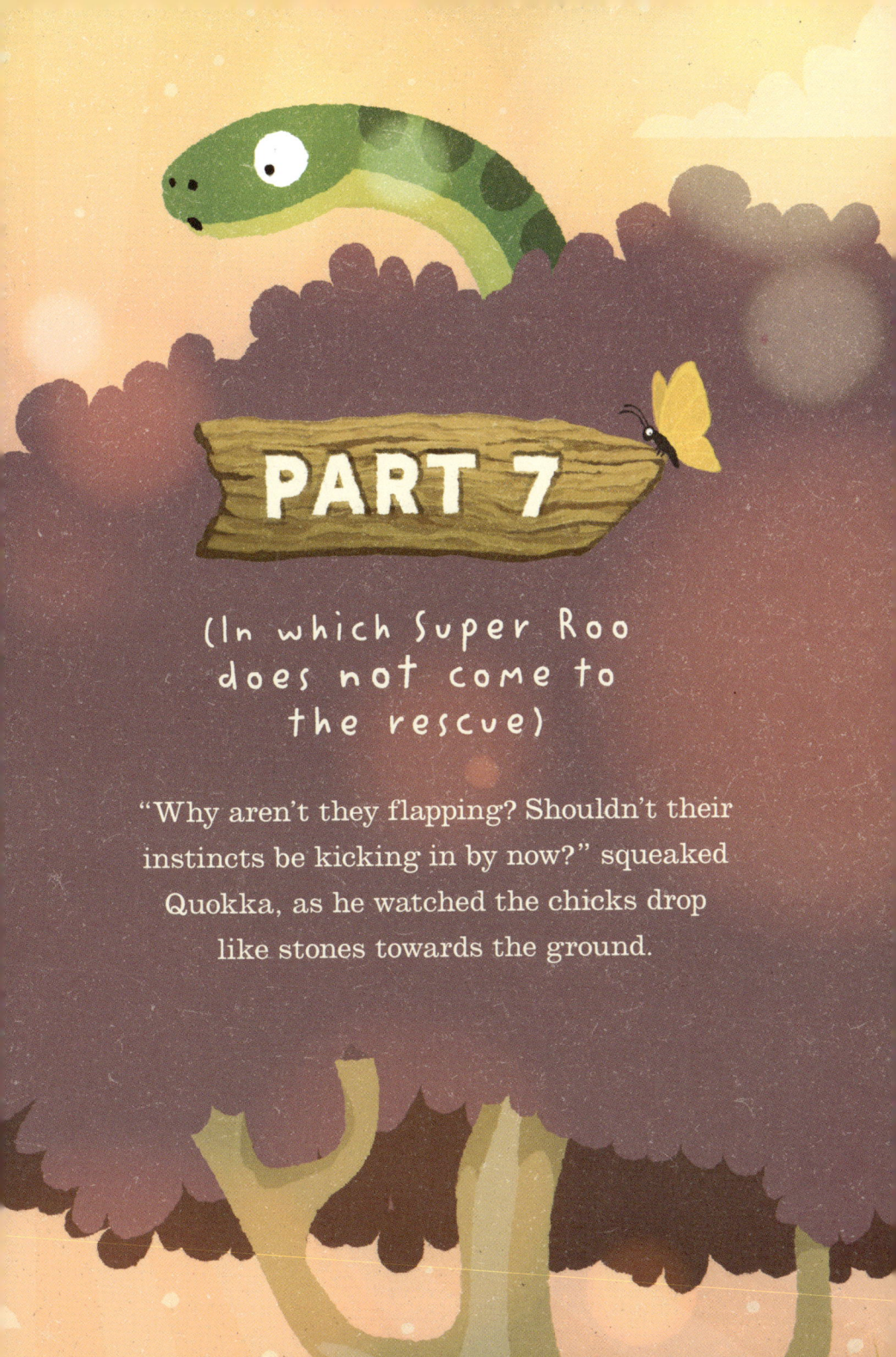

(In which Super Roo does not come to the rescue)

"Why aren't they flapping? Shouldn't their instincts be kicking in by now?" squeaked Quokka, as he watched the chicks drop like stones towards the ground.

Suddenly, the booming noise returned, louder than ever. Then, a monstrous blur of feathers came hurtling straight towards Wombat, Roo and Tree Roo.

"They can't fly!" shouted the giant bird. "They're cassowary chicks!" "How do you know?" said Wombat. "Because I'm their daddy!"

"Eeep!" squeaked Quokka, as Python squeezed her squealing snack.

Meanwhile, Tree Roo hadn't moved an inch.
"If you're so super, why aren't you helping?" said Wombat, crossly.
"I had a wash this morning," replied Tree Roo. "Don't want to get my fur dirty."

Roo looked at the scene in front of her and thought fast and hard. Then she leaned back onto her tail and t h u m p e d the trunk with her big strong legs until the whole tree shook.

Python clamped onto the branch with her jaws, but the swaying loosened her grip on Quokka.

"Aaaaaah!" shrieked Quokka as he slid down Python's back.

Wombat ran towards them then flipped over, letting the chicks and **Quokka** bounce off his soft belly just in time.

PART 8

(In which the chicks take flight)

The tiny chicks ran, cheeping wildly, towards the giant bird. They nuzzled heads gently.

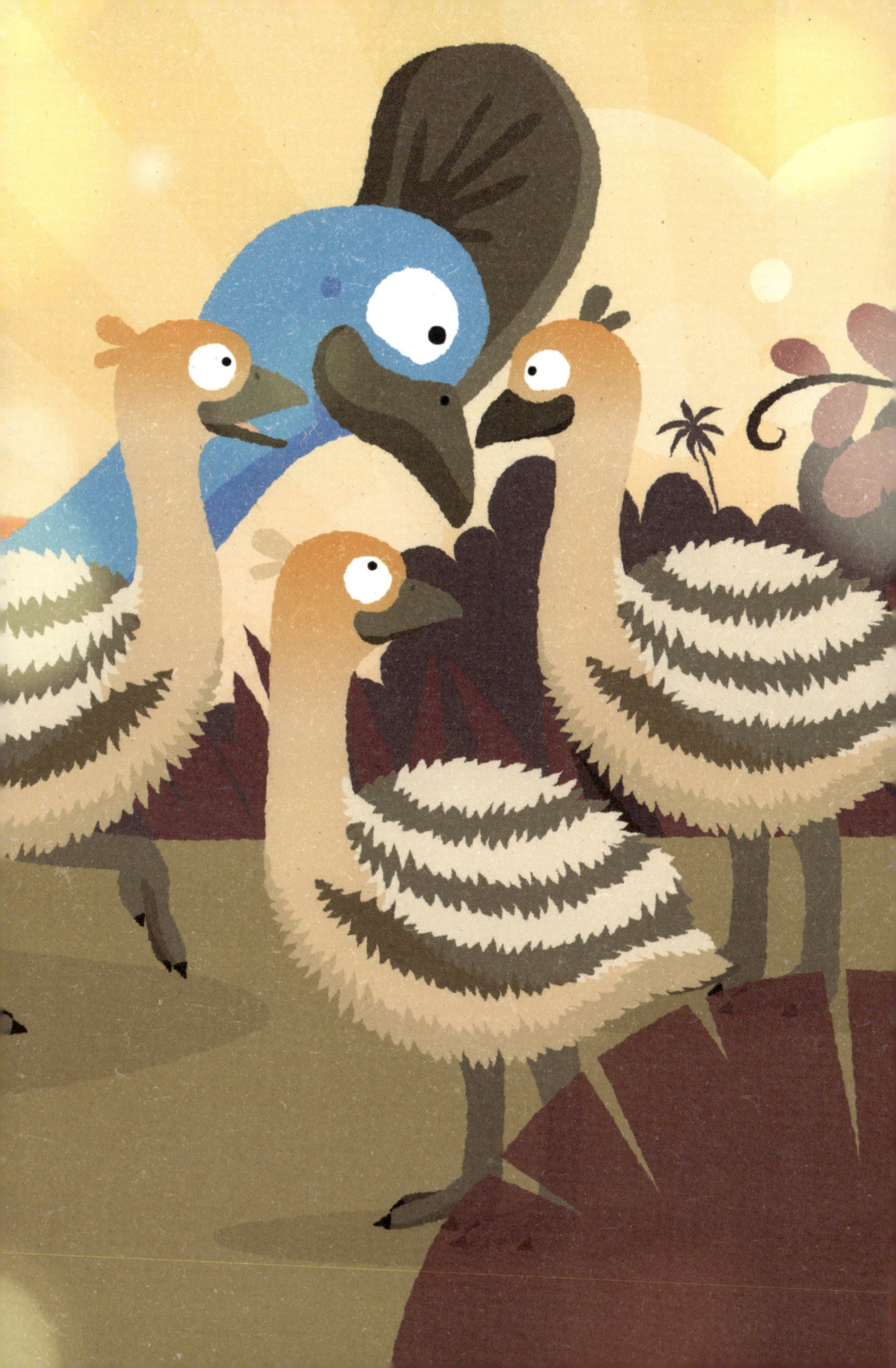

"The name's Daddy Cass," said the bird. "My girls tell me you found them and brought them home. Thank you."

"Yes," said Roo. "They were hiding in my pouch, a long way from here. How did they get so lost?"

"Let's just say that is the last time we play **hide-and-seek** for a while," he said.

Quokka stepped forward quietly, his head bowed low. "I'm very sorry I threw your chicks out of the tree. I was trying to save them. I thought all birds could fly."

"An honest mistake," said Daddy Cass forgivingly. "And yes, my girls would love to fly. They watch the kingfishers and ask me every day why they can't swoop and soar like their feathered friends. But our wings aren't even strong enough to blow away an ant's fart. I keep telling them we were born to do something even more magic than flying!"

"Ooh, I love magic!" said Quokka. "Show us! Show us!"

"It would be my pleasure!" said Daddy Cass. And with that, he pooped.

"Yeck! Please don't tell me you're going to pull a rabbit out of that!" said Quokka, holding his nose.

"Pooping isn't magic, everyone does it!" added Wombat. "Yours isn't even square!" he said, disapprovingly. "Ah, but our poop comes alive!" said Daddy Cass.

Wombat yelped, then scurried into the bushes, imagining the stinky pile suddenly transforming into a smelly little lifeform.

Roo noticed a fallen piece of fruit nearby, and began eating it, realising she'd forgotten to have lunch.

"If you watched it long enough," continued Daddy Cass, "it would grow into a tree and that tree would grow fruit. Fruit that wouldn't grow here if it weren't for us. Delicious fruit just like the one you are eating."

Hakuna matata.

The Stinky, Stinky Circle of Life.

Roo took a step away from the fruit.

"Cassowaries help to grow beautiful life-giving forests just like this one from our bottom," said Daddy Cass. "Isn't that magical?"

As they gazed at the wild and wonderful forest around them, they had to agree. It was magic. (Disgusting magic, but still magic).

The rest of the afternoon passed
in a happy Funcle-filled blur.

Grr!

Argh!
Argh!
Argh!

Ooh, more brownies.

Still no!

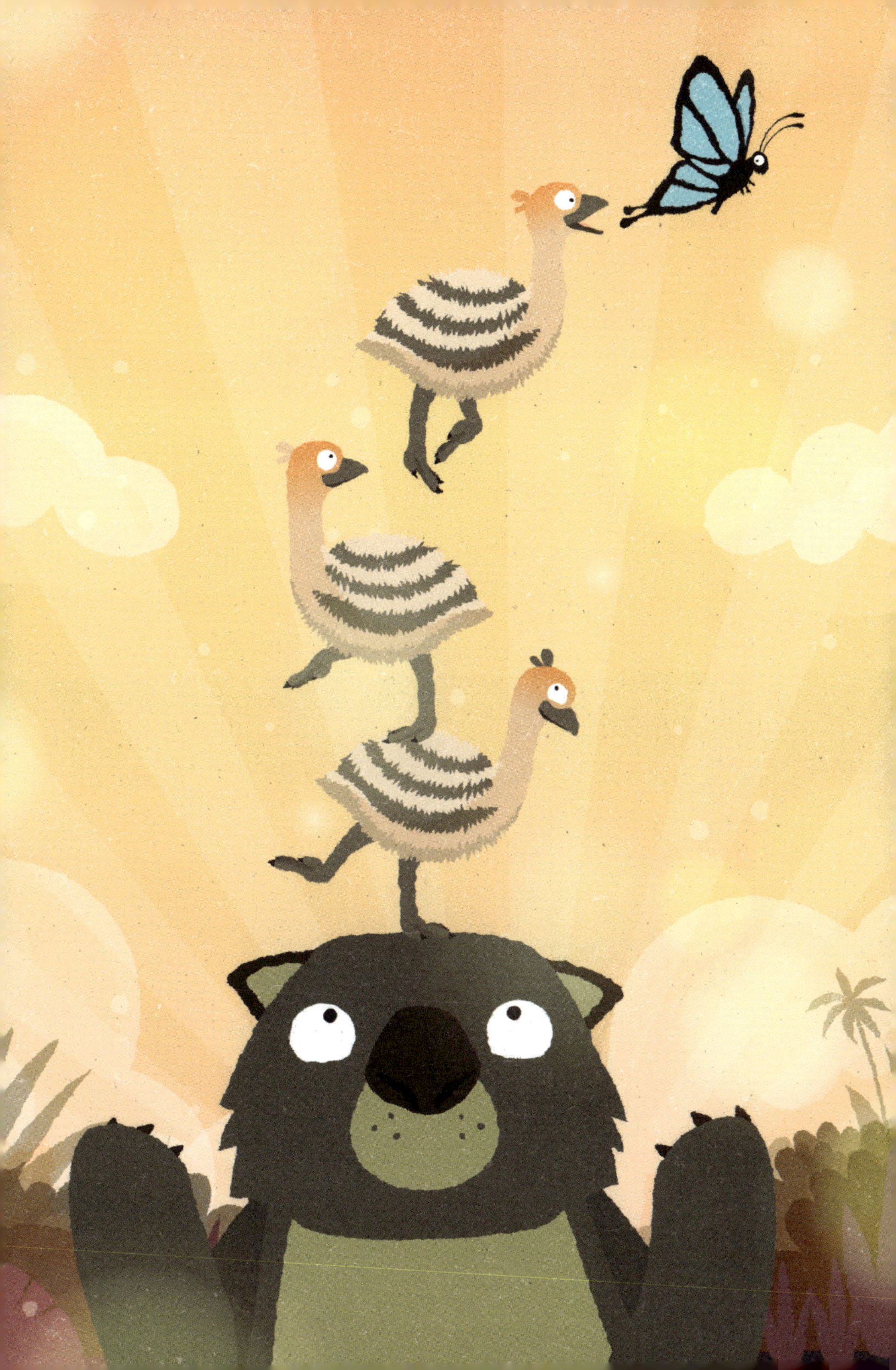

"I wish we could stay longer," said Wombat, "but it's getting late. We really should head off before it gets dark."

Roo watched Tree Roo scurry effortlessly up the tree and let out a long, sad sigh. "Are you okay?" asked Wombat.

"I would just really love to know what it feels like to climb a tree," said Roo wistfully. "And swing from branches. And walk backwards. But I don't have thumbs, or the right kind of legs. Sure, I'm good at hopping, but I guess I just wish I was a bit more Super, like Tree Roo."

"Tree Roo was pretty super," said Wombat. "Super rude, super selfish and super lazy! He did have some super skills, but he didn't care enough to use them.

Look, the chicks are home safe because we worked together, using the different strengths Nature gave us. Besides, Roo, you have a gift that is even more magic than tree climbing."

Just then, Roo noticed the chicks, perched on top of a log trying their hardest to fly off it. She felt a pull in her heart. She knew exactly how they felt.

Gently, she placed the chicks in her pouch and then she started bouncing. With each enormous leap the chicks felt like they were floating. No, not floating... Flying.

They darted with the dragonflies, cruised with the kingfishers and barrel-rolled with the butterflies. They whooped and whee'd as they felt the wind whistle past their ears.

As she listened to their thrilled shrieks,
Roo realised Wombat was right.
She didn't just have great big legs.
She also had a great big heart.
And together, that gave her a truly
super gift she wouldn't swap for anything.
Not even a Slightly Magical Bum.
Or a Very Excellent Thumb.

Eee!

The Free Range.
Lake Jabiru.
3
Quoll Hole.
Platypus Pond.
4
5
The Plains of Peril.
Monitor Marshes.
2
Owl Ave.
1
Wombat's Burrow.
The Mountain.
The Great Bullshark Bight.

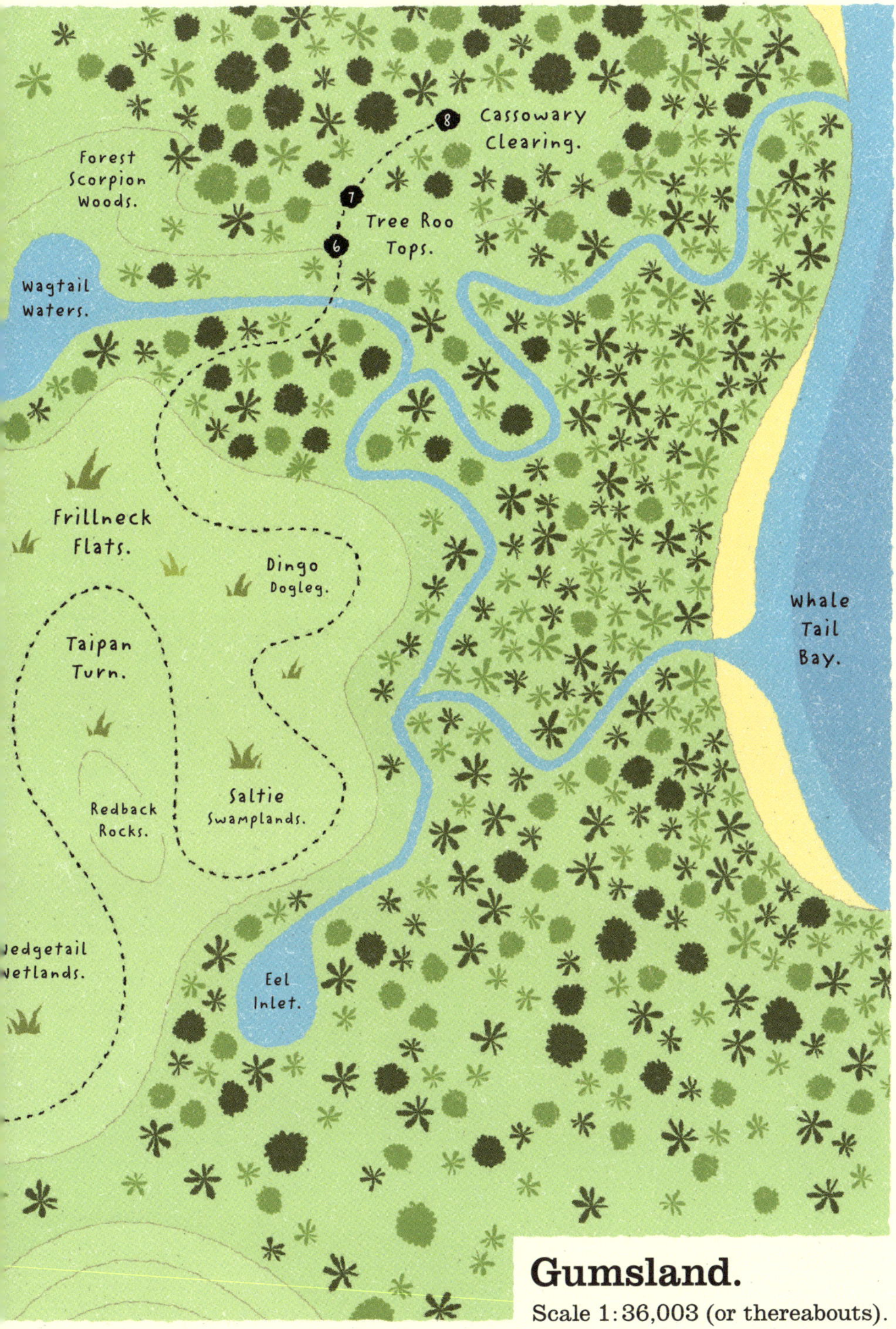

Gumsland.

Scale 1:36,003 (or thereabouts).

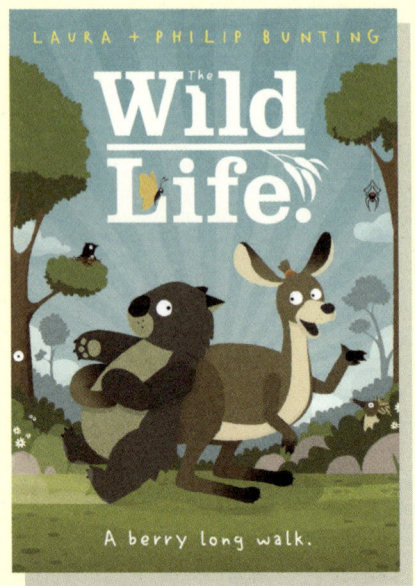

Book 1.

Book 2.

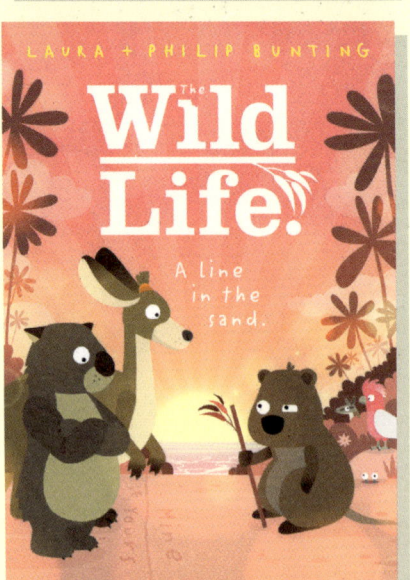

Eeeeeeee!